THOUGHTS FOR HAPPY LIVING

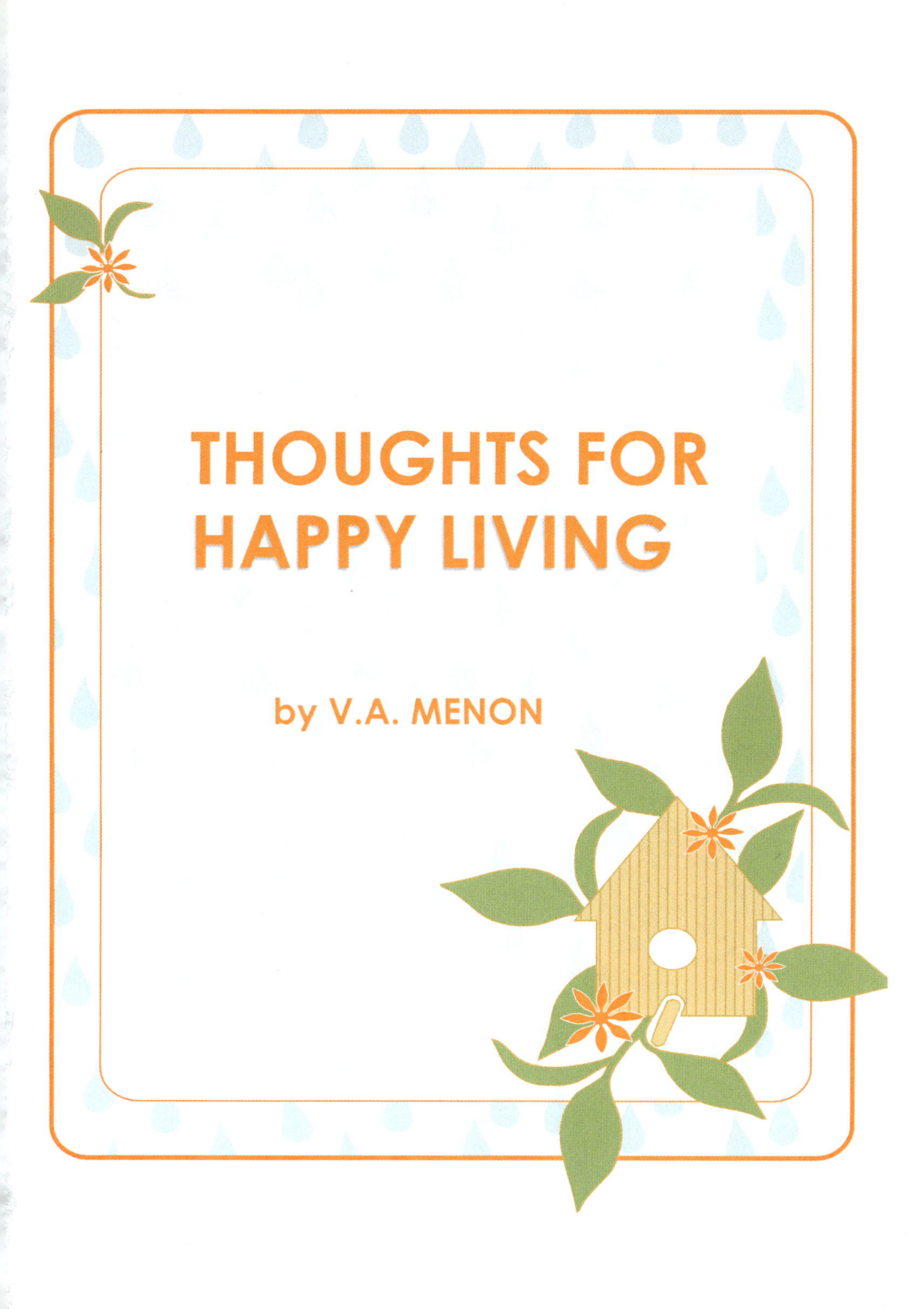

by V.A. MENON

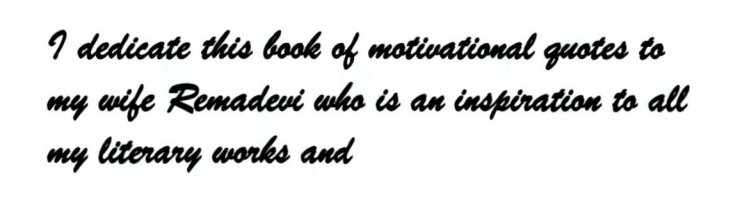

I dedicate this book of motivational quotes to my wife Remadevi who is an inspiration to all my literary works and

To my daughter Dr. Roopa Menon who has compiled these quotes.

On a hot summer day sit on a chair or sofa. Do not put on the fan. Close your eyes and imagine - you are walking through a forest. You walked for a long time. It's very hot. You start perspiring and you are thirsty. You check the bag. Water bottle is empty. No tap is found anywhere. You kept walking. Unbearable thirst. You are too tired. Suddenly you see a tent. You enter to find some water.

Inside on table you see lemon, water bottle and a bottle of sugar and no one around. You take a glass full of water. Cut and squeeze lemon and put some sugar and stir. Your mouth started salivating. You take the glass and start drinking...

Did you feel the taste of lemon juice though no lemon juice around? Like this your mind can go for a ride or someone can take it for a ride. Addiction to superstitious beliefs too can take you for a ride. Alcohol, narcotic drugs, cigarette etc. also can drive your mind. You become an uncontrollable victim. If you awaken your consciousness and conscience, you can control your mind, your habit and behavior patterns.

Before you start speaking you must ensure that you are a good listener. If you don't listen carefully, whatever you speak will be irrelevant and irrational. Keep your mind in rapt attention while you listen and never try to interrupt in between. After listening, think and evaluate all the points raised and then start speaking touching every point you listened. Don't speak or say any comment without judging circumstance and occasion. Your comments may be uncalled for. Speak only if it is better than keeping silent.

****

I am a scientist. And a scientist with deep fascination with physics, cosmology, the universe and the future of humanity. I was brought up by my parents to have an unwavering curiosity and, like my father, to reach and try to answer the many questions that science ask us. I have spent my life travelling across the universe, inside my mind", said Stephen Hawking. Did your parents encourage you to use your mind extensively to explore the expanse of knowledge? Are you encouraging your children to do so? Have an awakened mind, not a drowsy and sleepy one. Try to be a role model for people around you.

Can you always awake to the moment? When a crisis is happening in front of you, are you glued to your seat or jump and act? To jump and act you need presence of mind. To have presence of mind you need your mind always with you. If you keep sending it on tour, you will not have presence of mind. Father, mother sitting still on sofa when the child is about to fall, but grandmother jumps in and catches her. This is called alertness which everyone should have. Put off all automatic triggers and take over the control of your mind in your hands.

****

Confidence will power and courage to face challenges are not the gift of your heredity. It's developed through your upbringing. If your upbringing is with freedom, discipline and knowledge, you will have these qualities. Remove all negative conditionings, negative emotions from mind and imbibe it with freshness of wakefulness. Addiction to sleep will make you dormant and lethargic and will keep your spirit below average level. You will slowly turn good for nothing. Wake up and rejuvenate your mind by reading good books and acquiring knowledge. The more you climb up the ladder of wisdom, the more confident and vibrant you will be.

Do you say that people don't like you? If yes, then it's that you have not developed a likable nature. Your nature, attitude, behavior, habits etc. are developed through childhood by learning. Learning and brainwashing are different. Learning is a slow and systematic process. But brainwashing is forcibly imposing ideas on mind. Parents, relatives, friends do this. Whatever you learned can be changed. But it's difficult to change or wipe out whatever is imposed on mind through brainwashing through childhood. This will need your conscious effort. Your nature and behavior pattern etc. are based on these imposed ideas. These conditioned ideas will supersede your education and you will remain same irrespective of the high academic credentials you hold. You will be monitored by this mental conditioning and not by knowledge. Make conscious effort to change your mind to develop a likable personality. Live a wholesome life.

****

Don't do things or buy things to show others that you can afford them. People whom you display your lavishness to get their clap may be able to afford better things than you. They may be clapping at your foolishness. Do things and buy things only out of necessity and not for showing off. Material possessions do not make you great. But possession of a lovable and caring mind makes you exemplary.

Some people say that their married life is very happy and joyful. Husband, wife and children create heavenly bliss at home. But in many other cases husband and wife behave like rivals and children are crushed in between. Why? What can be causes?

In the beginning days of marriage, they say they are two bodies and one mind. Later both become two. Clash of ego, greed for money, lack of understanding, lack of free communication, refusal of sharing, Stubborn and adamant nature and mentality, addiction to superstitious beliefs, doubting nature and perverted and dirty habits are some of the causes.

One turns Master and treats other one as slave. Marriage can survive only if there is equality and uniformity in thinking. Free and frank discussion should settle all disputes.

No one should feel he/she is always right. Mutual respect and mutual compromise can keep relationship stronger.

****

The moment you identify yourself, the moment your mind is with you.... That's the moment of happiness in your life. Catch that moment and live with it.

Free your mind from all childhood brainwashing, all unscientific beliefs and superstitions and bondages of traditions and let your mind elevate with wisdom and freedom and you will find that it flies to eternal bliss and you will start seeing and experiencing goodness all around and you will start imparting love, care and goodness to all. A mind in prison can do nothing. A free mind can fly to intellectual wisdom. Then every word you speak and every action you do will be filled with positive energy and you become an asset to people around you. You will be able to touch the minds of everyone and they will start missing you when you are not around. A smile on your lips, a gesture on your face should spread wisdom and happiness around.

****

Do you feel you are the most knowledgeable person around? Are you adamant on your views and opinions? Do you try to impose your views on others? Do you keep boasting yourself and never give others to voice their views? Do you feel that you are always right? Are you a sleep addict? Do you have an unstable mind? Are you aggressive and victim of negative emotions like pride, jealousy, anger? Do you have habit of making comments without thinking?

If answer to these questions are "YES", then it's high time you seek a counselling help. Keep mind tuned with knowledge and activities. Don't leave empty space in your mind. Devils are waiting to enter.

In day to day life do you have anything creative or encouraging to talk other than the routine domestic things? If your children are around how do you interact with them? Is it only on their routine study topics which they must be bored off? What do you have to talk with them which they will be engrossed to listen? Are you blank? Then you have turned yourself into a zero by keeping yourself away from the ocean of knowledge around you. Check if you are an enemy of books and reading.

****

Marriage should be a contract of friendship and not of slavery. In friendship there is give and take, compromise, sharing, there is debate and argument but immediate settlement, there is no play of ego, there is equality. But in a contract of slavery there is only submission and surrender. One is master and other is slave. In friendship intelligence and wisdom play. In friendship there is a bond of love and caring. But in slavery there is only arrogance and ruling. Happiness, joy will linger around in friendship. Anger, negative emotions, ego will rule in bond of slavery.

Do you face problem in interacting or adjusting with others? Before finding fault with other's approach, why not check your own attitude? Many times, it's our attitude that creates hurdles on our way. We should change our behavior patterns, attitude, nature and beliefs to suite the changing world. Else we will land ourselves in the dust bin of history.

****

We enjoy and appreciate the beauty and elegance around us. But do we try to protect and retain it? Each one has a bit of responsibility in this issue. Try retaining the cleanliness and radiance around us. It will enhance our health and wellbeing.

****

Corona virus is invading the globe and trying to wipe out human race from the face of earth. The entire human race is shivering with fear as death toll keep rising. Everything including places of worship is facing lockdown. No magic, miracle or divine powers are helping us to survive. Only an effective vaccine can save humanity. Let us light a lamp to show our solidarity and respect to the Medical Scientists around the globe who are struggling day and night to invent an effective vaccine.

Your success will be in instilling inquisitiveness in your child so that every moment of life he/she remains motivated to do or achieve something new. His/her thinking faculty will remain awakened. But for all these your participation is vital. Spend quality time indoor and outdoor with your child. Keep answering all questions and encourage to ask more questions. Your brain should be a basic encyclopedia for the child. Don't go to google for help which the child can do himself. Google will not have the emotional bond to present the answer as you can do. Don't groom an engineer or Doctor but groom a genius who can create a tomorrow.

****

You always strive for total perfection in every item you buy. But do you keep yourself accountable for the work you do? Do you insist for total accuracy and perfection from yourself? Do you look for accuracy in your thinking and beliefs? Do you check for accuracy and clarity in your daily habit and behavior? Do you insist on quality assurance from others which you are not sure that you have it in yourself? Quality, perfection, accuracy etc. should start from you.

A state of being aware and responsive to surroundings is called consciousness. For consciousness to work, you need a physical brain. It's a game of neural connections done by neurotransmitters. Any energy cannot have consciousness as it does not have a brain. Software cannot function without a hardware. To send a WhatsApp or browse a video you need a laptop, mobile, iPad etc. The electrical energy cannot light a tube or rotate a fan unless you make it do using your consciousness or intelligence which are functions of brain. Energy can only act blindly like storm, cyclone, thunder--lightening etc. Every piece of matter has an inherent quality. In and out matter is in motion which is its quality. Change is another quality of matter. Matter is continuously changing. From non-living to living was a great leap. All planetary motions obey Newton's laws of motion.

****

The jasmine flowers blossomed in our own garden has no fragrance. But jasmine flowers blossomed in neighbor's garden has very good fragrance." This phrase is used to illustrate that we ignore many things which are near or in front of us which has enormous shine. We should not underestimate anything or anyone. When someone who was desperate in life going pillar to post for help and if you too ignored or avoided helping him, may one fine day see him reach a top position and you seek his help for a crisis in your life! Life is game of dice. Anything can happen to anyone. If you see a chance to help someone, never hesitate. A return on your gesture can Come to you from unexpected quarters.

Opposition should not be for just blindly opposing. It should be constructive. Person who opposes should have a valid viewpoint. Opposition should not be on emotional ground. It should lead to debate and discussion, not to arguments and quarrel. Each one should put forward his/her opinion with valid reasons. This can lead to the birth of new ideas. Discussions should be on subject or view which is substantially valid. For example, if you do a debate on how Covid 19 started, it will not end reasonably well as no one has any valid evidence on how it started though many hypothetical views are spreading on media. We should go by firsthand evidence, not by third party propaganda.

****

Are you getting fed up of your routine activities? It is natural to get bored if you keep doing same routine every day. Why not try to give a novelty to each day? Why not try bringing innovations to routine job? Look at a Master Chef. New innovations every day. New dishes, new taste. He enjoys each day. Try to be a different person every day. Different attitude, different behavior and different attire each day. Different topic to discuss, different title to read. Give a boost to each day.

Man's cruelty to nature has now put him indoors literally in-house arrest and nature is flourishing outside. Polluting air, water and environment, dumping waste into river, sea and roads, piling up of dumping grounds, massive use of non-degradable plastic, deforestation etc. were crime against nature. Now nature is hitting back. Man has created fertile ground for bacteria and virus to undergo mutation and new potent ones are taking birth. This is testing time to realize mistakes and start loving nature and its ecosystem. Respect symbiosis and start living with love for all living beings. We should remember that the universe is not human centric. Nature will only flourish without humans. We should try to save our own species. Man created lethal nuclear missiles and other weapons to eliminate his own species. Now he has no weapons to fight the new virus.

****

Do you buy a fifty-year-old car for your daily use? If you are a collector of antique items, you may buy it. But not for using it. You will go for the latest model. If this is so, why do you go by the information, predictions written in centuries old books written at a time when advancement of knowledge was negligible? It certainly has a historic value and tell us about the life and culture of people of a bygone era. Why not go by the updated latest information? Try taking your mind forward, don't back date it to past centuries. Keep auto update feature active in your mind. Allow new information to come in and wipe away the obsolete old ones.

When you reach old age and when you look back you will find it difficult to remember how all these years have passed. Did you utilize your bygone years creatively? What's your asset today which your children can be proud of to present you in front of their friends? Only bank balance?

If you don't have any hobbies, you will find it distressing to pass time. Other than all the biological activities which even all other animals do, what's your achievement as a human being who owns the most sophisticated machine in the world - the Brain? Did you use it effectively and efficiently or just kept it as a museum piece and slept away all the time? If yes, then you will be struggling with generation gap.

As days, months and years pass in front of you, don't alienate yourself from the vast ocean of knowledge. Keep your friendship with BOOKS alive and ensure that you remain mentally young always. Like your body needs exercise to keep fit, your brain cells too need activation to be alert. Reading, music, art, painting... there are a lot of things that can keep you engaged in old age. Try to be a living encyclopedia to the little ones around.

You cannot be an Einstein, but you can certainly think like Einstein.

When you face a problem what you do generally? You will run pillar to post for solution. Say some one fall sick, we try all local remedies first, then go for remedies advised by neighbors and then by friends. When nothing works, we go to doctor. By the time it may be too late. Even Doctor may not be able to help. When we face a problem, we should target for expert solution. Immediately rush to the expert in the field. We live in a world where there is an explosion of knowledge. We should gain at least primary awareness of each field so that no one can take us for a ride. Having medical awareness is a must. This will help us to seek right advice at right place and right time. When we fall sick if we don't go for immediate medical help, not only that we will suffer, but also pass it on to others around us. Let us be socially conscious.

****

Are you a mobile addict gulping down everything that are flashed in YouTube and WhatsApp? Then you are loading your mind with numerous unverified dummy information and rumors. When you come across an information, you should do investigation to ascertain its accuracy. If you are unable to do verification, it's better to ignore it. You should not turn someone else's view as your own view without ascertaining accuracy. Always go for your own firsthand verification instead of accepting the result of a third-party verification which also may be incorrect. Always use scientific method for verification. Generally, many people accept many things they hear or come across as fact then ask others to confirm their acceptance. Instead one should verify to ascertain accuracy. If you have a logical mind, it will help you in every walk of life

Are you using your abilities to the maximum? Have you measured what's your stretchable limit? Our brain is not set for multitasking. It cannot do more than two function at a time.

When two functions are given, brain divides it to two hemispheres. When it must handle one single function, both hemispheres together participate, and the function is done well. This is important when you allocate work to your subordinates. Don't overload with multiple tasks. Their efficiency and overall perfection will go down.

When you handle multiple activities, you are likely to forget some, and your concentration to each activity will be less and your overall efficiency goes down. Always make habit of using a diary for making notes.

All cells in your brain is always working. The more you concentrate or divert your attention to an activity; the best will be your success.

Every individual has different levels of brain power and each one's stretchable limit too will vary. You must tune up your mind to reach your level of optimum performance.

Yesterday is gone. You cannot get it back. You are one day old today. Many changes have taken place in your body. Many cells have died, and many new cells have grown. Your hair has grown a few millimeters. Nails have grown. Same way your mind too is older by one day. Your level of thinking and maturity may be different from yesterday. Today is not the day for correcting yesterday's mistakes and blunders. It's a day to create and achieve new horizons. Just ignore or forget what happened yesterday. If you had any argument or verbal clash with someone yesterday, today is the day to ignore the past and join for a better today. Today should tune you up for a lively tomorrow.

****

It's morning. You have refreshed your body by taking a refreshing bath and having a hot cup of Tea. But is your mind fresh? Is it still in the hangovers of yesterday? Did you refresh it from yesterday's stress? If not, your today cannot go smooth. Sit relaxed in a silent room and keep your mind totally blank. No thought should come to mind. Now do breathing exercise for ten minutes. Breath in through one nostril closing other one with finger, hold the breath till you can and then breath out through another nostril. Now repeat with another nostril. This increases your oxygen intake and supply of more oxygen to brain cells. Play light, pleasant music at home. Start the day with happiness and joy. This can strengthen you to meet the challenges waiting for you.

Just reading books is not the only way of learning. That can be a method of study to score marks or grade. Learning is a process of understanding nature. If you have flare for learning, nature will unravel in front of you. There is knowledge all around you. Everything you see, everything you use daily has many things to tell you. Keep your mind open. Keep learning and updating and correcting yourself. What you know or what you learned need not be correct. Unlearn to learn again. When knowledge expands and explodes in mind one can get intuitions. It is this intuition that leads to innovation and discoveries. When a commander controlling aircraft or surgeon performing a complicated surgery or soldier on the war front when met with a crisis, his intuition guides him. Just memorizing textbook lessons, one may not get intuitions. Even common man can get intuitions at times to come out of a difficult situation. It all depends on the tuning up of your commonsense which helps to keep presence of mind sharp.

****

For any problem there must be a solution. How to find the best solution depends on your approach to the problem. If your approach is aggressive and spontaneous, then your search for solution also will be like that and the solution will be short lived. Problem will strike you again. Patiently study the problem and look for accurate and permanent solution. Never go hyper on problem or solution. Maintain a scientific approach to everything. Cool and pleasant mind and a smiling face will always keep you composed, and you will find everything around you turning for better.

To face challenges is the biggest challenge in everyone's lives. There is always victory at the other end. It's your dedication, sincerity and courage to face situations that will make the difference. Don't let your laziness or your inherited blind faiths hold you back. Look at a small child. When it tries to get up and walk, it falls and gets hurt many times. But keeps trying again and again till it succeeds. Means you got to learn from child. All innovations and discoveries that we see around are made by handful of people who never got tired of struggling. Why not wakeup to the dawn on achieving. There is fun in moving against storm.

****

Students are worried about carrier choices. First know yourself, your strength, values, personality and skills. This will help you to decide which choice best fits you. Take five sheets of paper. On each sheet write the name of one field you like to choose. Now you have five Carrier options on five sheets. Now under each name write five reasons for choosing that field. After filling all the five career sheets, start evaluating one sheet per day. Evaluate all pros and cons, expense other difficulties etc. and write on the sheet. Start eliminating one by one which you feel not fitting. On fifth day you will be ready with your final choice. Your choice should be fitting your taste and not fitting your parent's status or ambitions. Your career should give you not only money but also satisfaction and happiness.

It took millions of years of evolution to transform single cell organism to human beings. Again, it took millions of years of further evolution to evolve human brain. Again, it took thousands of years for the social evolution of mankind. Organized social life of man has revolutionized and modernized the world. Evolution from actions and sound into spoken language made all the difference. Man lived through combating natural calamities. This gave rise to fear and man conceived the concept of a superpower to help him. But only his struggle and courage helped him to live ahead. Even today only his intellect is helping him to find a way out when attacked by problems.

****

Years back I saw a road show in the fort area. A man was sitting fully covered with black cloth and the moderator was continuously speaking to him and the public assembled. The man under the black cloth was doing predictions. But you should tell your question to the moderator first. He would loudly read the questions and man inside will answer. To my surprise I saw he predicted the number of a currency note. Every day I used to stand and observe for some time. First two days I did not follow anything. Then I keenly concentrated on the dialogs of moderator and observed that at the end of each word he spoke he added an alphabet. The man inside joins these alphabets and speaks out as predictions.

Common sense is something which many people lacks. Even highly learned people or high degree holders also fall victim to rumors spread on social media. We should not easily gulp everything that comes in media. Don't rely on anything just because you feel it came from a reliable source or best friend. Either ignore them or go to investigate and get firsthand information. Always have a skeptical mind, not a believing and accepting mind. Don't spend hours on mobile checking YouTube, WhatsApp etc. and satisfy that you have lot of knowledge. All can be fake. Only reliable sources are experts in the respective fields and books.

****

For every good or bad happens in your life praise and blame should go to your mentality first. Blame yourself before blaming others. Suspicion and misunderstanding are the main causes behind many domestic quarrels and fight amongst friends. Suspicion will keep expanding in mind and turn you to schizophrenic and you start visualizing that people are doing things against you. When Suspicion strikes your mind, kick it out by free and frank discussion. Ignore all negative things you come across or try correcting them. Never keep your mind blank so that anyone can enter and reside. Fill it with positive thoughts. If you have positive thoughts, you will have positive attitude.

Give and take should be the motto in friendship and in family life. The moment you get married all " I" should become "we". "Mine" should become "ours". Everywhere it should be joined opinion. Understanding should be given priority over misunderstanding. Free and frank discussion should be daily feature. Marriage should be a contract of friendship not of slavery. If you are highly self-centered, proud and dominating, it's better you lead your life alone as bachelor. Marriage is a divine association of two likeminded people. Don't pollute it with your vulgar habits and perversions. Your face is the mirror of your mind. Let others look at your face and decide what you are.

****

If you reach the height of intellectual wisdom, you will turn down to earth simple. You will start enjoying and appreciating the beauty and wonders of nature. Your every action and every word you speak will be refined. Your intellect will reflect in your behavior and interactions. Only reading and logical thinking can lead you to intellectual wisdom.

Your individuality and personality are the result of your mindset. There are people who look and behave highly dignified manner out in public, but at home very perverted and misbehaving. This is example of split personality. Most of such problems are due to bad upbringing. Highly pampered child can turn like this in adulthood. They will be of confusing nature and getting hyper and angry and next moment start crying for their fault. They are poor victims of altered mentality badly needing psychiatric assistance. Don't look in the mirror. Look at yourself and ascertain how you are. In and out of home you should be dignified. Your behavior and habit patterns should be normal and refined

****

Your opinions should be based on logical thinking. If not, all your opinions will backfire on you. You should keep all your moods, whimsical attitudes and aggressive temper with you. They will have no market. Your social involvement and interaction also should be based on clear thoughts. Your presence should make others happy and your absence should be felt by them. Your presence will be felt by your virtues, not by your personal getup.

Small doses of liquor slowly turn into many pegs and then into full bottle, and mind turns into a property of alcohol and full life the addict lives without own mind, a life worse than that of any other creatures. Other creatures never get addicted. Similarly, superstitious beliefs fed into child's mind by parents and other relatives slowly takes over his/her mind and he/she turns into a lifelong victim. Mind becomes so sick that without adhering to such beliefs he/she does not get peace. Here you can see a person who does not have any control over his mind.

****

Addiction to superstitious beliefs turn you into a mental pervert. It's worse than alcohol addiction. Here the mind is sick 24x7. And you will try to forcibly pass on this addiction to others. Use conscious effort to free your mind from this prison. Else seek psychiatric assistance. Only a free mind can fly up to the height of intellectual wisdom. Only intellectual wisdom can prove that you belong to the species Homo sapiens.

You should be watchful of your child's behavior and habit patterns as he grows up. Child has a lot of free time. He can go naughty or start doing perverted things. Some parents proudly say their child is very naughty, throwing and breaking things and bitterly crying when demand is not met. These are problems, not qualities to be proud of. Take away all free time from your child. Engage him in some or other activities. Give lot of toys/colorful books as per age. Join him/her in all household activities like housekeeping, cleaning, cooking etc. Boys also should learn kitchen work. I have seen small children organizing delicate glass items in showcases with care. Hats off to their parents.

****

If you give guitar to a musician, you can listen to melodious music. But if you give it to a common man what can you listen? Children born to intelligent and cultured parents go to heights. You need to reform yourself before you decide to have children. Your children should be proud of you before you can be proud of them.

Disciplined behavior should move with your child wherever he goes. It should move with you when you travel to adulthood. In many houses I have seen that children are better role models than parents. They are self-disciplined geniuses. Your mode of life, pattern of behavior, talking and personal habits should change for better when a child arrives. There should not be quarrels or high pitch talking which can instill fear in child. Nature has given a delicate brain in your hands. Handle with extra care. You can turn this delicate brain to a super genius of tomorrow. Provide encouraging visual and auditory stimuli. Child needs your care, not your ruling.

****

How to do character molding of children? Culture and behavior patterns cannot be spoon-fed. Child can learn these only through illustration, means you must illustrate it at home. Cool and responsible behavior, communication, lovable environment are the essentials at home. Many parents complain that their son was spoiled by his friends. But if their son was good, then why he did not make his friends good? No one care to analyse. I stayed with bachelor friends who everyday joined together for liquor party. I had told them that I am personally against drinks. Then they never bothered to invite me. If you have a heritage, you can pass it on. If you don't have, then you will become a victim.

There is always opposite for everything. There is opposite side for a coin. There is happiness behind every pain, success behind every failure, rejoicing behind every depression, day behind night, waves are not nonstop, rain or wind too are not continuous. There is a stop just behind evert start. There is an end just behind every beginning. Everything that begins must end. Kill your ego and move ahead to see a better opposite. Life, happiness, joy and health are in your hands. Mold your mind for a better molding of yourself. Mind your mind and then everything will be okay in your life.

****

Most of the obstacles to clear thinking are due to the following.

LAZINESS TO READ

INCORRECT LOGIC

INCORRECT PERCEPTION

RIGID THINKING

Evaluate which is affecting your thinking.

When you visit a monument what you generally do? Just see around, take selfie or photos and come back. Here you don't learn anything. Say you are at Taj Mahal. As the guide explains the history, make your mind go to the era of Emperor Shah Jahan, imagine you are among common people moving around during that time and now listening to the guide see all around you. You will really get a feel of that bygone era. You can visualize the life of people of those times and the thousands of slaves who worked hard to build Taj Mahal.

****

Usually you learn through printed books. But there is a book which you can never finish reading. It's NATURE. It's geography, the varieties of plant and animal life, the aquatic life, the interstellar cosmos, the climate variations, time zones, natural monuments, man-made monuments .... There are unending things to learn. The more you learn, the more you will find which you are yet to learn. Encourage your children to learn nature. Take them on picnic to the abundance of nature. Learning is a process of acquiring knowledge, not just a tool to get a job.

Whenever any calamity strikes the world you will read in the media a lot of predictions. They say they predicted these years back. People who readily accept such predictions fail to ask the following questions. Did he predict the exact time and date of the starting of the event? If it's a disease name and age of the first person who suffered and exact time and date when he recovered or died. Male, female or child. Number of people suffered the world over. Number of males, females and children and each one's correct age and their location and country. Number of people died. How may males, females, and children and their age location and country. Did he predict correct cure or medicine?

****

All predictions are mentally conjured. Inanimate objects in the cosmos has no role in the illnesses spreading in the world. But man has a direct role. Man is destroying his eco system. He does deforestation, pollution and global warming is on the rise. Bacteria and virus keep undergoing mutation and new stronger ones are coming up. Our erratic use of medication too has a major role to play. Due to this, germs are turning resistant to medication. It's time to look at our own actions and not to predictions.

With lock down in many countries, air quality is improved, and birds and butterflies are coming out in large numbers. Seashores have no human presence. Dolphins are playing on top. Sea lions are playing on the shore. Animals are freely roaming in the forest without fear. Nature is enjoying the absence of its destroyer. Its time man learnt a lesson that without nature he can't survive.

****

Sit on the chair near your study/worktable. Place a sheet of white paper on the table. Open a micro tip gel pen and lightly touch the tip on the paper. Now close your eyes and continuously think strongly that you are writing an alphabet you thought of. After a minute open your eyes. You will see that you have written something without consciously moving your hand. Your thought has transcribed into action. Your endorphin system has made your hand move without your knowledge. Many things you do without your conscious knowledge. Many professionals use this feature to take you for a ride. Mass hysteria, communal violence etc. gets created like this. Don't let your mind go out of your hand.

What is happiness? It's not something that you can acquire from outside. It's also not available online. Your happiness should come from within you. This will happen if you have positive attitude and mindset. Happiness can reside only in a peaceful and calm mind. Drive your mind yourself and attain happiness. A happy mind is an enlightened mind. Only knowledge can reside there. Just empty your mind of all garbage and fill with knowledge.

****

Having a skeptical mind is an asset. This will help you in every walk of life. What you see, hear or read can be misleading. Nothing should be taken seriously until you ascertain the truth yourself. Don't go for public opinion to clear your doubt but go for expert opinion. One who knows that he knows is great. One who does not know that he does not know is a fool. Which category do you belong?

****

What others tell or advice are their views. Most of these views may not be their own. They must have borrowed it from others. Don't mute your brain and go by here say. It's your birth right to go by your own views. Never lose this right. Let your own mind throw light on every issue. Go with truth and reality not with predictions. No one has any power to predict. It's all hypothetical, conceived by minds.

When you get up in the morning, don't anticipate that the day is going to be all yours and everything that happens will be for good. Use your full mental and physical energy to turn the day for you. Remain composed and bear a smiling face to turn adverse occasions in your favor. Life is not a bed of roses. But your will power and dedication can make it. Don't see what others are thinking and doing. Concentrate on what you should think and do. Don't get moved by praise or blame. Always keep yourself in your own control.

****

Learning is the process by which your mind expands. It starts from the moment the child is born. Child learns through observation. As the child grows her inquisitiveness increases and start coming to us with questions. Don't underestimate child's grasping or understanding power. We should give correct answers to every question. Learning is not just to pass exams; it should be an ongoing activity to advance our mental horizon and our personality. Just like your body needs exercise to retain health, brain cells too need exercise to remain active. Make reading a lifetime hobby.

None of our five senses are reliable. They can be cheated. That's how we can enjoy films and magic shows. People who claim miracle or divine powers are doing the same. No human being has any special powers other than the intellectual ability or the ability to cheat others. Whenever we hear or see any mysterious things, we should investigate to find the truth. We should use our common sense and logical thinking power. We should use scientific method to analyze. Mental blindness is worse than visual blindness. We should brighten up our intelligence by continuous reading and logical thinking.

****

Every belief is result of fear. No belief is true. We don't say that we believe we have mother, father etc. because they are there in front of us. In other case something is not there but we believe it's there. This happens because we don't allow our intelligence to function. Intelligence does not believe anything. It always like to explore to find truth. Allow your intelligence to function. Nature has given you intelligence to use. Don't keep it locked.

When your child achieves something, making a painting, creating a craft work or writing an essay, are you praising her telling "Great. You have done the best". If you say this, then you are putting a limit to her creativity. Instead if you tell, "you have definitely done a good job. But see if you can do still better." Here you are invoking her creativity and inquisitiveness. Never use superlatives to praise your child. In any job there is still a scope for improvement. Nothing is ultimate.

****

How do you plan your child's future? Is it by booking admission in a high-profile school with heavy donation and fees? Are you using heavy pressure on him to compete with others to score high grades? Are you scheduling all his waking hours for studies? If answer to these questions are "yes", then you are grooming a robot or a bonsai at home. Here you are ignoring nature. Nature gives a lot of potential to each child. We should identify these by allowing the child to grow naturally without external pressure. We must just encourage and monitor child's nature given talents by looking to child's patterns of play, actions, taste etc. and groom accordingly. When nature wanted him to be a singer, don't turn him into a doctor or engineer and vice versa.

What did you do for yourself today? How much could you improve yourself? Your behavior pattern, your habits, your public interaction.... are all these same as yesterday? If yes, then you did nothing for yourself. You simply let the day pass in front of you. Changing or upgrading yourself will be your great achievement. At the end of the day evaluate yourself. A mirror can reflect your outer figure. Look inwards to see your real figure. Try to present a better "YOU" tomorrow.

****

Make learning a pleasure for children. Create love for books from early formative years. Learning should be made a routine activity without attaching any extra importance tag. Child should realize that it's his job and it's for him. If this is done, then parents' interference will be needed only for getting admission and buying books and gadgets. Make home a place for lively discussions and debates. Find time to be with children. Make him compete with himself and not with others. Take him to outing to beaches, parks, forest areas, book fares etc. Encourage him to make creative friends and do group learning. Invite his friends' home occasionally. Above all be good role models in front of him.

When the child reaches the age of three and half, he/she is put into prison by parents. In the prison of education, the child suffocates. All the talents and brain power given by nature vanishes from him. He becomes a tool for parents' ambitions and prestige. School, classes, special tuition... His day gets full. No play time, no social mingling... It's mechanical life for him. Only concentration is on his grade. He is groomed as a Bonsai or Robot. Growing without attachment to parents, family or friends, when grown up, he sends parents to old age home and start grooming his kids in the same manner. Are you a parent in this group? Then it's time to change your attitude. Make learning a pleasure, not punishment.

****

Man has accumulated defense artillery and nuclear weapons to destroy enemy nations whose inhabitants are our own species. Human beings are the only creatures who exploit and destroy own species. Now real enemy is attacking the total human race. It's the invisible, microscopic Corona virus. And we have no weapon against it!

A play (Drama) will be nice and enjoyable if all actors do their roles well. Our life will be successful and happy if we play our role correctly, as life too is a drama. You may be wife, husband, father, son, brother, sister, grandpa or granny. Are you playing your assigned role correctly? If yes, then your life and living will be smooth and happy. Everything turns miserable when you alter your role. Learn the screen play well and understand your role and play.

****

Childhood is the time one can master language skills. Your children should be exposed to all possible languages. Open all arenas of knowledge in front of your children. Don't put their mind to prison. Don't cut their intellectual growth. Don't turn your child to a Bonsai.

****

If you are in love with knowledge, your graph of progress, your personality and your individuality will keep going up. Knowledge does not fall from nowhere. You can acquire it if you are in constant love with BOOKS and reading. Allow the fragrance of knowledge elevates your wisdom to groom you into a socially useful individual.

It's always good to have your own opinion on everything. But never be adamant that your opinions are correct and never try to impose it on others. It's possible that your views could be totally wrong. Always evaluate yourself, analyses yourself and try changing yourself before trying to change others. Many conflicts arise because we try to rule others with our opinion the accuracy of which we ourselves are not sure about. We should respect other's point of view also. We should liberate our mind from all sort of conditionings. Have a stable mood and don't allow it to swing.

****

When you wake up in the morning, can you tell Good Morning to yourself? Did you wake up to new morning or are you still in the hangover of yesterday? Yesterday can take you backwards, but today can give you momentum to move ahead. Tune-up your mind for a bright Today.

****

There is no positive or negative energy around you. If you Tune-up your mind to think positive, you can be self-motivated to achieve. Motivation does not come from outside. It's something you must self-create. Don't let your mind fly high with imagination and don't let it acquire more weight than other minds around you.

Satisfaction and contentment are reflection of our mind in return to our actions. When we do shopping, when we sell some item or do any action if we don't keep our greed and other emotions away, we can never be satisfied. We will always feel, "I could have done better", "I should have got more", "what I bought is not good let me go and change". These are symptoms of anxiety. We have made our mind sick. This will not happen if we use our conscious efforts. Then we will feel, "what I did is my best", "what I got is the best I can get". Don't move around with sleepy and lethargic mind. Be conscious always.

****

Your life can take a positive turn if you can implement in your life at least fifty percent of what you suggest and advice others to do.

****

Try Pranayama and Raja yoga (meditation) for a change. Try bringing mind to total silence to wipe out all negative thoughts. Try brainwashing yourself against all negativity.

Human beings who live in various regions of earth have different skin colors due to climatic variations. They developed different lifestyles, different food habits, different spoken languages, different types of clothing and different cultures and habits. All accept and accommodate these variations. Then why people are not ready to accept the differences in religious beliefs? People developed different beliefs and formed different religions. If we accept the differences in beliefs, there will not be any rift or enmity. Though there are differences, all are human beings. If we honor this single fact, everyone on earth can live with peace and harmony.

****

When you take a refreshing bath all impurities from your body gets washed out. Brushing with a good toothpaste will remove all impurities from your mouth. But how about the impurities accumulated in your mind like negative thoughts, pride, jealousy, hatred? Does a head bath wash out all these? Can a dip in a holy river do this job? All negative emotions in mind keep crushing your body and body gets prone to various diseases. How can you eliminate all these and bring happiness? Can devotion or prayer help? If yes, world would have become a better place century back.

Are you living your life just because you are alive, or do you assign any purpose to it? We have come to the world accidentally without any purpose. But we have a choice-- we can just live and die an idle life, or we can live a meaningful and purposeful life. We can assign a purpose to our life. We should see what we can do to the family, to the surroundings and to the world in general. For this we should turn ourselves literate and meaningful. Let's try living a wholesome life.

****

Let your mind be controlled by knowledge and logical thinking and not by superstitious beliefs. Don't degrade yourself by admitting that you are superstitious. Change your mind set, muster courage to wipe out all illogical beliefs from your mind. Bring your mind from primitive era to modern world. Be a modern human being living in modern era.

Difference of opinion and arguments are part of life. Arguments should lead to healthy debates and not to enmity. It's from debates new opinions and findings come out. When in argument keep mind cool and don't allow adrenaline level rise which can raise your blood pressure. When you keep mind in control, you will get positive points to sustain your point. Remember that you need not be correct always. List out proof and reasons to prove you are correct. If you cannot, agree with opposite party and withdraw. This should be true even in home front. Arguments should not lead to domestic violence and divorce etc. Even at the end of argument friendship or love between both should be intact and should sit together for a cup of Tea.

****

Our face is the mirror of our mind. Every emotion affecting mind will be visible on our face. There are people who has trained themselves as expert mind readers. They are called mentalists. Looking at every movement on your face they can find what emotion is affecting you. With their communication skill they will make you reveal many things without your conscious knowledge. They can take over your subconscious mind for some time. Astrologers, fortune tellers and many others have this expertise. Love at first sight, friendship at first meeting etc. happens like this. Basically, you are giving away your mind. Many cyber cheatings happen like this. Listening to sweet talk over phone, people reveal their card OTP, PIN etc. and get their account wiped out.

Everything in the universe is changing. Only thing that doesn't change is change itself. Generations are coming and going. Are you keeping pace with the changes around you? When you vanish from the world you will leave behind all the material gains you amassed which others will use and finish. But if you leave an intellectual legacy, it will remain forever. To elevate yourself intellectually, you must read, think, analyses and evaluate. Google can give you information which is in its database. It cannot teach you anything new. But you can research and develop new things and ideas. Keep using your brain. Keep gaining new knowledge and keep passing on to others around you.

****

We should not look at things with preconceived ideas. Many preconceived ideas and beliefs are always haunting most people. This is due to brainwashing from childhood. Vaastu sastra, astrology, palmistry, tarot card, planchet etc. are blindly accepted by lot of people though these do not have any scientific basis. Those who practice these use various methods to influence people. Those who are afraid due to indoctrination from formative years fall easy victims. Even high degree holders are victims of unscientific ideas. If everyone looks at things with free mind and evaluate using scientific method, they can identify truth from falsehood.

When you laugh, there may be hundreds to laugh with you. But when you cry, only your shadow will be with you. Happiness can be shared, not sorrow. Unexpected situations in life can make you sad. In most cases it may be your inability to find solution which makes situation worse. Happiness can exist only in a peaceful mind. Depression, sorrow etc. come to agitated mind. Learn to keep your mind calm and free from wild imaginations. Unlearn all habits and beliefs you learned from childhood and learn again with rational thinking. Think a moment before every action and speech. Keep your subconscious mind at rest and make consciousness and rapt attention to guide you. A spoken word cannot be withdrawn as it creates impact on the listener. Your words can impart happiness too.

****

We always make a mistake of looking at things from our point of view. We ignore other's point of view. This leads to dispute and quarrels. We forget to consider the fact that our view may be wrong. We should never try to impose our habits or views on others especially children. Children should be encouraged to develop their own views. Never try to make them lifetime prisoner of our views. They should grow to be independent personalities, not as our carbon copies.

Reading is the only way to acquire knowledge. We are different from other living beings only because of our highly evolved nervous system. Are we using it to its maximum level? Our body remain healthy if we do regular exercise. Our brain cells too need exercise to remain active and healthy. Reading is the best exercise for brain cells. It will keep Alzheimer's away from you. The total stored data base in your brain cells is your mind. Don't be lethargic, invigorate your brain cells and expand the horizons of your mind. Make reading a regular habit.

****

Are you good at quick decision making, or getting confused on and off? What we need is stable mind at every moment of the day. To have a stable mind you need consistency in thinking. You must be quick to evaluate the pros and cons of what you are going to do. Once decided, stay with it. Logical thinking and positive attitude can help you in this.

A few hours of peaceful sleep can rejuvenate you and you will be happy and cheerful. A day full of positive thinking, good and successful activities can give you sound sleep. Sleep will avoid coming to a stressful and agitated mind. Sleep has various stages. hypnosis, rapid eye movement sleep, catalepsy etc. Hypnosis is a state between wakefulness and sleep. Many centers of brain will be awake and many in sleep in this state. Whatever you reinstate in your mind in this state can make changes in you. Tell yourself that you are healthy, stress free and joyful. And wake up to a pleasant morning. When you don't feel sleepy, start doing some activities like reading or listening to light music.

****

When you are in acute distress or crisis, if you can remain composed and calm, you will be able to find a solution. Stress can only make you sick. Thinking can work only in a calm mind. Wild imagination can come to an agitated mind. A school bus met with an accident and stopped on roadside. Children came out and started playing. Someone phoned one of the parents that school bus met with an accident. The mother fainted and fell. After a few hours' child came home, but mother was in ICU. Stress will kill your thinking faculty. Train your mind to be cool even in worst situation.

Are you a victim of superstitious beliefs, surge of emotions? In fact, you are a slave of your mind. Without your conscious knowledge your mind is forcing you to accept and do things. You are worried about Astrologer's predictions, the directions you sleep and keep things, the time you do things...and many like this. Though all these are meaningless and illogical, your mind is restless if you don't obey these. All these are due to the reinforcement done on your mind from formative years. Unless your conscious mind overrules the subconscious, you cannot escape from these. To give power to your conscious mind you need scientific literacy, not simple literacy. You must bring your mind to your conscious control.

****

How organized are you in life? Are you in the habit of haphazardly keeping or throwing things here and there and afterwards spending stressful days to locate an important item? When you give a doctor's prescription to a medical store, within minutes the pharmacist brings you the medicine. This is possible because all medicines are systematically organized in the store. Similarly, your home and your place of work should be properly organized. How to utilize a minimum space to maximum use will be your brilliance.

Every man-made machine comes with a user manual. But the most sophisticated and most complex natural machine - the human brain which got developed on its own through millions of years of evolution does not come with a user manual. You must create your own. People who create good user manual goes to heights to become scientists, musicians, artists, singers etc. Those who creates bad user manual turns to be dacoits, fanatics, terrorists etc. Don't try making manual for your children. Guide them to make their own.

****

What you read and see in media is someone's opinion. Don't make it your opinion. Give your mind and intellect a chance. Investigate and verify yourself. What is written in centuries old books need not be true. Verify with current available knowledge before making it your views. Don't accept any views blindly just because someone you feel great has said. We should love and respect our parents and seniors and great people but need not respect or accept their views blindly as their views may be obsolete and not in tune with current knowledge. We should elevate ourselves with our own individuality which should be integrated with modern knowledge. Spectrum of knowledge is advancing. Let's not keep our mind shut.

Brain is not mind. The total recorded information makes up our mind. Brain is only a hardware through which mind works. A child is born with an empty brain. It will have only some inborn traits. It's the environment, parents, teachers, friends and people around fills child's brain and mind gets formed. This is like you add software to a computer. Scientists have recovered children groomed by wolf, monkeys etc. They were walking on four legs and knew no language, no knowledge. No information recording in the brain. We should play positive role in developing children's mind. Don't pass on information which we are not sure about accuracy. Don't assume you are right. Use scientific method to verify. Don't go by propaganda or writings on media. Investigate yourself to find the truth.

****

People believe in many paranormal happenings. There is a science dealing with this called "parapsychology. Telepathy, telekinesis, ghosts, premonition, rebirth.... are some of the areas dealt by parapsychology? Modern science does not agree with parapsychology as its research is not based on objective truths. One can simply believe and accept anything on its face value. It's the easiest activity and most people go by this. But if you like to know the truth behind something, you need to verify, investigate, analyses and bring out concrete proof and evidence. This is a difficult task compared to blind acceptance. Only investigation can open new vistas in knowledge.

Once ex-students came to meet professor. Professor solved their problems quickly when they were his students. Now they have lucrative jobs, bank balance. But no happiness. Why? Professor brought them tea in different type of mugs. Some were steel mugs, others porcelain mugs with multi-colour artwork. Students took tea kept in porcelain mugs. None of them took tea kept in steel mugs. "Why none of you took tea in steel mugs? Tea was the same in all mugs?" asked professor. He continued, "Life is like this. Your job, profession, flat, money are things to make your life happy. But you give more importance to these than your life. That's your failure. Give importance to all aspects of your life. Then you will be happy.

****

If you can't understand something or a phenomenon, it doesn't mean it's something divine or a miracle. Someone else may be able to understand them. If no one can understand, then it should be treated as a mystery which needs enquiry and investigation. Universe is full of mysteries. Many mysteries we unraveled through scientific investigation. Many we are still trying. If we treat something as divine or a miracle, then we are putting a full stop to investigation. That will be the end of knowledge and we will remain in mental darkness. There is an ocean of knowledge around us. Let us keep our mind open to it.

It took billions of years for modern man to evolve through organic evolution. It again took millions of years for the evolution of human brain. As generations go ahead brain cells undergo mutation and evolution continues. It is through years of evolution individual man turned into social man. From sign language to spoken words it was a great leap for human race. Man kept on making advancements using his innovative and intellectual skills. But even in this advanced era we see that human thinking remains backward. This is due generations of mental slavery. Superstitious beliefs and rituals are imposed from day one the child is born, and enslavement continues.

****

Don't see wild dreams about tomorrow ignoring today. Today is at your disposal, tomorrow is not. Achieve your maximum today. How you manage your today will decide your tomorrow.

****

SILENCE...... practice it when you get agitated... When you get angry.... When you are stressed.... When you are tired.
Keep your mind silent for at least 15 minutes in the morning and before sleep. Sit relaxed, close your eyes, remove all thoughts from mind, keep mind blank and concentrate on your breath... count down from 100 to 1. If you happen to fall asleep, wakeup and count from beginning. This will refresh and rejuvenate your mind.

What we need is not literacy, but scientific literacy. We can see even highly learned people highly superstitious. They lack scientific literacy. A person with scientific literacy can be a person who may be having just basic school education. But he will stand far superior to the high degree holders. He will have positive attitude towards life, society as he is possessing a logical mindset which is not prone to blind beliefs. Elevate your children's mind towards scientific temper. Groom them to be makers of tomorrow.

****

Birth is not our choice, but living is our choice. Live a meaningful life which is full of enthusiasm. Our life turns meaningful when it turns meaningful to others. When people around you turns happy in your company and misses you when they are away, you can be sure you achieved something. What elevates you is not your degrees or positions, but what image you made in other's minds. Once the number 1 was proud that it had a value compared to zero. **Zero** came and stood on the left side of 1. 1 laughed at the valueless zero. Suddenly zero went and stood at right side of 1. 1 now went speechless. It's no more 1. It's 10 now. Never assume any head weight and be proud. Be humble and humane. Your value and greatness are in what others think of you.

Belief puts an end to your inquisitiveness and enquiry. It keeps you in a world of wild imagination and you become victim of many illogical practices. For example, a person who believes in auspicious time will be desperate in doing things within that time. If he fails to do, he turns tense and sick. He loses logical mind to understand that there is nothing auspitious about all 24 hours of the day. Believing mind is literally a sick mind where even psychiatry cannot help as it is conditioned from childhood. Throughout life they remain prisoners of their own beliefs and all the doors of mind remain shut to the advancing knowledge.

****

Is rebirth a fact? Yes. But it's not after death. You are reborn every day. When you get up in the morning you are one day older. Lot of cells in your body have died and a lot of new ones have grown. Your mind too will be different from the previous day. Visualize the new yourself, rejuvenate, wakeup to a brighter morning with more enthusiasm. Live with enthusiasm to wake up to a new life next day.

Learning should not be restricted to books alone. There are lot to learn from nature and people around you. Observe nature carefully, see the variety of plants, birds, animals and other creatures and their living and migration patterns. Learn from history of peoples who made history. Good observation, patience to listen, enthusiasm to understand are qualities needed for learning. Learn from the daily items you use like say currency notes. What are the languages and monuments printed on it? Learn nature and working of gadgets used daily. Learning has no limit or end. If you encounter a question or an event, don't assume answer. Use scientific method and logical reasoning to find answers.

****

Do you have a regular excuse that you forgot? Whatever you do with an alert mind you will remember. But what you do with a sleepy or absent mind you are most likely to forget. Human brain can store over 100 trillion bits of information. Brain activities are carried out by electrical impulses travelling down the long fibers of each cell through the release of neurotransmitters. These chemicals play vital role in information storage. Intellectual stimulation can keep memory at its peak. Human brain can remember only one out of every 100 pieces of information it receives. Keep your mind always alert. Document every information on your diary. Don't depend on your mind for everything.

Each one of us like to be happy always. What is happiness? It's the relaxed state of mind where endorphin levels are balanced, mind is fully relieved from stress and thoughts and is in your total conscious control. How to achieve this? When you see a good comedy film you become happy. But you cannot keep seeing films. When you eat a favorite food, you are happy. But to extend happiness you cannot keep eating. Then how to be happy always? Happiness is generated by your own mind, not by outside agencies. These agencies are just sources. Keep your mind calm, don't let it travel to stressful areas. If your mind is peaceful, you will experience happiness which will reflect on your face.

****

Are you fan of a film star, politician or some Guru? When you are fanning the greatness of someone else, you fail to identify the greatness hiding in you. All the people whom you consider great, were fan of themselves. They could identify their own talents and raise to greatness. Blind fan worship is one of the worst social evils. Whatever the leader or Guru orders, the followers blindly obey without thinking if it's correct or not. Mentally the followers become slaves. We should admire and appreciate the greatness of others but should not become their blind fans. Why don't we try to be our own fans and raise to greatness? Let us be intellectually bright and not intellectually bankrupt.

Do you have a believing Brain or a thinking brain? If you have a believing brain, you will accept and agree with any event that happens in front of you or any hearsay or rumors that's in circulation without any verification. You will move with centuries old beliefs, traditions and many will proudly say that they are superstitious. They don't find any shame in proclaiming their mental backwardness. But if you have a thinking brain, you will verify everything before accepting. This is scientific approach. Scientific approach can put you on the path of progress and help you to keep your mind in current century.

****

What makes you great is not your material possessions. It's the culture and virtues you hold makes you great. These cannot be spoon-fed to your child. She should pick from her home. Your home should have the magnetic power to keep your child attached. Wherever she is, she should be tempted to come back home. Such a home is a real heaven. Parents should be good guides not rulers. Evaluate the air quality of your home. Is the index of culture and virtues high? As the child climbs the ladder of progress, she should turn more and more humble and humane and should be spreading the fragrance of her home.

It's human inquisitiveness which is responsible for all the innovations we see today. As generations go ahead brain cells are undergoing mutation and as a result innovation are coming up. Look at a child who is coming to you with questions. Are you equipped to satisfy the child's inquisitiveness? Remember, this child can be a future asset to human race. Always give correct answers to his/her questions. If you don't know correct answer, guide him to the source of correct answer. Don't underestimate child's ability to grasp or understand. He is equipped with a brain more advanced than yours. Remember he is one generation ahead of you.

****

Do you have presence of mind? This is something that can help you during difficult times. How to achieve this? For this you need peace of mind. If you have a wandering mind, you cannot have peaceful mind. Bring mind to your conscious control and don't let it be carried away by numerous thoughts. Doing meditation can help you achieve a stable mind. Emotions will not rule over a stable mind. Every living being on earth face problems. Observe a dog sleeping in your compound. Don't think it's sleeping peacefully. Anytime a stone can fall on it. Even in sleep it's always alert to get up and run. Why we humans are not alert to situations? Because we fail to achieve stable mind.

Never consider yourself as inferior or superior to anyone. No one is superior or inferior to anyone. All are different from each other. You are unique to yourself. Never try to compare yourself with anyone. Only two similar qualities can be compared. You can compare sweetness of Alphonso mangoes with sweetness of other mangoes. But you cannot compare it with fragrance of a jasmine flower. You can certainly compare yesterday's yourself with todays. Do you find any change or improvement? If yes, then you can hope to see a better you tomorrow.

****

Are you letting your mind go haywire? It may go nonstop and can put you in depression or psychosis. Put your mind under your conscious control and don't surrender it to outside agencies. It's your precious possession. When a child is born, it's parents' great role to mound his mind. The information's coming into his brain through his five senses getting stored in brain cells which latter forms his mind. Ensure that correct information's are passed on to him. Ensure that he is exposed to Books and knowledge. Also, to good music and art. Remember, mind should be guided and controlled by logical reasoning and not by emotions.

How will be your future? How will be your tomorrow? Inanimate Stars or planets in the sky cannot decide your tomorrow. But your interactions to your surroundings, your behavior patterns, your actions, your motivation, your hard work etc. can decide this. No Astrologer can tell your tomorrow because he doesn't know his own. But if you are motivated by intelligence and brilliance and if you are guided by your own conscious mind, you can predict your tomorrow. Ask yourself how your tomorrow will be. Tomorrow will be there to those who act and not to those who idle.

****

Will a person who is happy, healthy and rich go to an Astrologer to find out when bad time is going to fall on him? Such a person will never go. But people who are struggling with multiple problems in life rush to Astrologers to find when they can see an end to their problems. Astrologer can read their stress on their face and does predictions to satisfy their faith and they get ready to do all what he says. After all the struggle when they are back, problems which they didn't solve strike them again. They failed to acquire mental strength to solve their problems which Astrologers do not provide. Only you can solve your problems. Acquire mental strength to kickout each problem you face.

People say they don't have time for anything. But we should realize that there are 24 hours in a day. Are we scheduling our activities correctly? We should not let time go out of our hands and don't let time use us. We should use time. We achieve when we are awake. We should not sleep away our time. We should not allow our mind to go gloomy or lethargic. We must keep refreshing it with knowledge. We are living in an ocean of advancing knowledge. We should not let ourselves get alienated from it. Let's move with time and try to climb up the ladder of progress.

****

Your life is a precious gift of nature. Try living a quality life as it is your only chance. Nature doesn't offer a second chance. Rebirth and after life are only an imagination. Don't surrender your life to things like cigarettes, liquor or to superstitious beliefs. Put life under your conscious control. Only then it can benefit you and the world around you.

All are worried about air quality and pollution which is eating away our health. But do we realize that the worst form of pollution is mental pollution which gives rise to all other pollutions? It divides humans into warring groups which tries to revolt and kill each other. Religious enmity, terrorism, violence etc. are increasing day by day. Peace and harmony are endangered items. Millions are spent on amassing weapons not because we have any threat from aliens, but to eliminate our own species. World need the birth of a new generation with stable and rational thinking mindset.

****

There are no bad people in the world. What is good or bad with them is the way they think and behave. If the mind is conditioned correctly, no one can go bad. All fanaticism, racism, terrorism etc. are creations of perverted minds. Weapons cannot go and wage a war. It's fanatic minds' political will that creates enmity and war. If a child is born to you, ensure correct development of his/her mind.

****

Are you an emotional bomb exploding on and off? Try formatting your mind and condition it with knowledge and logical thinking. This will help you to lead a meaningful life.

Continuous change and updating will refine our personality. If you say, "I am like this only, I will not change", then you are worse than other living beings. Even birds migrate to other places when climate becomes extreme. Animals too keep moving. Everything in the world is changing. If you are against change then you will land in the dust bin of history. Your thinking, your behavior, the way you talk and present yourself, the manner you dress.... everything should change with the change of time and advancement of civilization. Don't live in 21st century keeping your mind in stone age.

****

In humans walking is not an inborn trait. It's a learnt activity. Child start walking by seeing others walk and by getting assistance from elders. All behavior patterns, culture etc. are also picked up from parents who are role models Infront of them. Tune yourself to be good role models before planning to have children. Create healthy, harmonious, jovial, rational and loving environment at home. Create healthy and creative discussions and debates at home. Dismiss quarrels, rivalry, nepotism, egoism, pride, jealousy etc. from home.

****

Where there is opinion, there will be difference of opinion. Where there is understanding, there can be misunderstanding too. Only logical thinking can help us to be together. We should be rational in every aspect of life. Our every action should be motivated by a purpose. We all are humans, but to be humane is most vital.

Learning is a process that starts from the moment we are born. There must be a conducive environment for the continuation of learning process. When there is an alteration of the environment, the learning process gets upset. Learning should be for the continuous acquirement of knowledge. It's a process which should continue till the end of our life. But unfortunately for many it's just a tool to get a job, after which it gets alienated from their life. And their intellectual life ends here. Continue learning to keep mind vibrant and elite.

****

Spoken word is a powerful tool. It can be a magic wand to cure a patient. It can also make a person sick. It can make friends as well as enemies. Think many times before uttering words. We should ensure that words are coming from our conscious mind. Speak only if you feel it is better than keeping silent. Rhythmic chanting of religious prayer, vibrant and magnetic oratory by leaders can create mass hysteria. Here people lose control of their conscious mind and behave hysterically. A negative prediction by a fortune teller can make person sick and even lead him to suicide or death. Words are more powerful than any other weapon.

Are you setting the speed of your mind more than the speed of the activity you have started? You keep bucket under the tap and start filling water. But you are impatient because time is passing but bucket is not filling. But if you move out after opening the tap and start doing something else, you will find that water start overflowing. In first case the speed of your mind was more than the speed of water flow. In second case you diverted your mind to some other activity. The speed of water flow was the same. Don't let your mind move faster than the speed of your activity. That can give you stress and frustration.

****

It's nighttime. Dinner is over. What's next? Just go sleep. Of course, you must sleep. But before that spend a few minutes to see your balance sheet for the day. What all the good and right things you have done and what all bad and wrong things you did? This evaluation will help you to reduce your bad deeds in the next day.

What is the environment revolving inside your home? Emotional or intellectual? If it's emotional, then there will be constant unrest and unhappiness. If it's intellectual, then there will be peace and happiness. Living in this environment children will grow to heights. If your mind is conditioned with knowledge, then there will be no space for negative emotions. Don't leave any empty space in your mind. Keep reading and fill your mind with knowledge. Create environment for free and fearless debate and discussion at home.

****

Anyone can touch someone else's feet. But touching someone's mind is not easy. To get a place in someone's mind you must raise up yourself with virtues, intellect, refinement of behavior. These qualities will not fall from sky. You must inculcate yourself. Free your mind from all childhood conditioning, blind beliefs and elevate your mind to freedom and let the sparkle come visible on your face. This will make people to feel like meeting you again.

****

Look at the mirror. Can you identify yourself? Is the same 'you' of yesterday? Now look inward at the mirror of your mind. Now what identity can you find? A well-balanced human being or an emotional bomb which keep exploding on and off?

Groom your child to grow with intellect and not with emotions. If your mind is ruling you, you will be easily getting angry, depressed, sad. If you have grown with intellect, your mind will be controlled by you and then emotions will not rule you. Take charge of your mind. Victory over your mind will be your greatest achievement. Put your mind on silent mode for half an hour in the morning and night. Keep it totally free from all thoughts. Fill your mind with knowledge. Make reading a regular habit. If you are an enemy of books, then you will be a bundle of bad emotions and negative thoughts. Empty mind is always a devil workshop.

****

Mental slavery is the worst form of slavery in which outside agencies and objects are playing with your mind. Here you totally loose conscious control of your mind and you turn a victim. Look at a smoker. Initially he starts smoking but later cigarettes start smoking him. He turns a slave to cigarettes. He loses his integrity, self-esteem as one cigarette start dominating him. Same is the case with an alcoholic. It's utter slavery. Look at yourself. Are you able to identify yourself?

Ideal parenting does not mean that you should impose your beliefs, ideas and views on children. You should realize that your child is endowed with a brain that has undergone mutation which will be more advanced compared with your brain. As generation goes ahead Brain cells undergoes mutation. You should provide a wholesome and peaceful home environment where child's talents awaken. Do not underestimate their talents. You should be a guiding light, not an imposing authority. Child should be free to express their views. They should look at things through their mind and eyes and not through your mind and eyes.

****

We all spend a lot of money to do shopping for many of our festivals and home celebrations like Birthday. We buy lot of dresses, sweets, Tabs, mobiles for children. But how many of us spend money to buy Books for children? We take children to holiday resorts, parks etc. But how many of us spend time to take children to Libraries or Book fares? Are we keeping children away from knowledge?

****

When you start speaking or behaving look inward and evaluate your educational status, your integration, prestige of your family. Don't tag words with anger or insult. If you do, you will be degrading yourself and not the listener. Speaker forgets what he spoke with emotion, but listener remembers. Your behavior reflects your personality.

Switching off TV, hiding laptop, Tab etc. just because child is studying, or exams are near is an irresponsible act by parents. Study and exams should be the sole responsibility of the student and not parents. Mold them to realize their responsibility should start from day one the child is born. Don't be a remote control to discipline your child. Mold them to be independent and active. Allow them to be part of every home activities like cooking, housekeeping, cleaning etc. Treat them like adults and speak to them in responsible and creative manner. Create love for books and reading from initial formative years by giving them colorful books and telling stories and history of great people. Engage them in educational games by providing educational toys. As time grows, they will realize that reading and studying are their need. Then they will do it with sincerity and dedication and parent's interference will not be needed. Always try to keep home environment happy and cheerful. Encourage free and creative discussions at home. Children should be free and fearless to speak and present their views. Don't discourage their choices without valid reason. If you get angry with your child, he should be told the reason for it. Don't have dispute or violent argument with your partner Infront of children. Schedule it for a different occasion when children are not around. Children learn about loving and caring when they see it between parents. Don't let your child have any free time. Free time can make them naughty. Fill their free time with activities. Spend creative time with children every day. Plan occasional outing with your children to zoological parks, places with natural beauty, libraries, book fairs and shopping malls. Your child comes from your heredity. He is unique and don't compare with other children who are from heredity of someone else.

Education can be defined as modification of behavior. Teachers and parents instill in knowledge and child's mind start expanding. As the child's spectrum of knowledge widens, his pattern of behavior also changes. Knowledge creates more refinement in character and the way he socializes. Continuous reading and understanding continuously changes his approach to life and living. His words or actions will be different from an illiterate person.

****

Spoken word is a powerful tool. A few pacifying words can give relief to a patient. A few words of encouragement can give motivation to a student. A few angry words can cause fight between two people. A few negative words can spoil a relation forever. We should ensure that every word we speak should be intellectually monitored by our conscious mind. Our culture, integration, intellectual status should reflect in every word we speak. We should remember that every word we write or speak and each of our action will demonstrate our personality and the heritage we are from.

****

Look at the bird you just caged. It is making frantic attempt to fly to freedom. After years of caging the bird's brain turns conditioned and enslaved. Now if you open the cage it will not fly away. Same is the case with our mind. It is conditioned and enslaved since years. It cannot enjoy freedom. Bondages of religious beliefs, enslavement to many external outfits conditioned our mind. It's full of sorrow, hatred, jealousy, ego and the like. We are unable to own or control our mind, instead our mind starts dictating us. We are just victims. Do not try to condition or enslave you children's minds. Let them fly to freedom and experience happiness.

When you discuss or argue, are you engaging your conscious mind or just shooting words? If you win an argument with your oratory skill, it is victory of your skill and not victory of truth. To know or understand truth you should be on the path of knowledge. Read, think, enquire. Have a critical mind and not a believing and accepting mind. If you start believing and agreeing with everything that you come across, then you will always be a victim. For a change why not try logical thinking?

****

If you keep yourself depressed about your yesterday, you will lose your today. If you keep yourself worried about your tomorrow, then also you will lose your today. Instead take lessons from your yesterday and keep yourself ready to welcome your tomorrow. Tomorrow should not be your concern, but it should be your milestone. You should decide your tomorrow using your intellect and effort. Don't let any fortune-teller decide your tomorrow. Your tomorrow will be great only if your today is great. Don't be in competition with others. Be in competition with yourself. Keep evaluating yourself. Keep criticizing yourself and then you will keep improving and developing yourself.

****

When we have a question or when we encounter a mysterious event, we generally form our own answer. We never try for correct answer. Instead we try for the confirmation of the answer which we our self-formed. This will keep us away from correct answer. One who is inquisitive will not believe or assume anything. He will always be a seeker of truth.

Look at the smiling happy face of your little one. Don't allow her smile to fade away by imposing heavy disciplines, your ambitions, emotions and beliefs on her. Don't overload her with pressures of education. Learning should be made joyful to children. Love for books and reading should be created from early formative years. This will prepare them to learn without any pressure. Every child is a rare gift of nature born with many talents and potentials. If they are living in wholesome and free environments, they can grow to intellectual heights.

Are your children very naughty? Don't encourage or ignore it. Consider it as a problem and take corrective action. They are naughty because they have ample free time. Take out the free time from them by engaging them in creative activities. Give them creative toys, colorful books. Take them to educational tours to museums, zoo, parks, science centers, book exhibitions etc. Create a healthy and intellectual environment at home. Mentally come down to their level to talk and discuss with them. Your continuous interaction can tune them towards intellectual pursuits. Above all ensure that you are an ideal role model Infront of them

****
****

Knowledge will not fall into mind from sky. It must be acquired. Reading, observing and analyzing are the ways to expand your knowledge. All nature given talents will vanish into oblivion if you don't read.

There is happiness when mind is peaceful and surrounding is peaceful. There is happiness in sharing love and care. Happiness is a feeling given to you by your mind. If you have control over your mind, you can be happy always.

****

Nature has given carrier choices to your children. Don't try to overrule it and impose your prestige and ambitions on them. Identify what talents and abilities nature has given them and groom them accordingly. Remember you as parents are their first Teachers and role models. Play your role correctly.

****

You should lock in your mind the sweet memories of love and togetherness of first few weeks of your wedded life... This will be a strong repellent to all differences and rifts that may arise between you and will keep you together always. Remember, togetherness is the bond of your humanness and caring.

How much percentage of your mind is owned by you? How much percentage of it you have indented to outside agencies like religions, politics, blind beliefs, saints etc.? Some of these outside agencies can rule your mind and make you to dance to their tune and you become a victim. Your success in life will dependent on how much of your mind is with you. Your victory over your mind is your greatest achievement. Try to own your mind fully. Then your mind will start enjoying freedom.

****

Eating food is the time we are serving ourselves. All other things we do are to obtain food. So, we should be sincere and respectful for this occasion. Sit together with all and have only light and jovial talk not heated arguments while having food. Eat slowly enjoying taste of each items. Remember your mind should know you are eating. Then only digestive enzymes will be released correctly. Concentrate your attention on food and don't let your mind wander. After finishing don't jump out. Sit for a while as your saliva finishes digestion process. Keep your mind stress free and happy during the entire time. This will help proper digestion as glands will release correct quantity of enzymes.

Baby elephant is tied with a strong rope or chain which it cannot break. As time goes ahead a conditioned reflex is formed in its mind that it cannot break the chain. An adult elephant is tied with a chain which it can easily break. But it does not break and run away. This is due to the mental conditioning. Similarly, we condition our children's mind with obsolete religious beliefs and traditions right from the day of birth. When they grow up, they remain victims of this conditioning.

****

We keep upgrading things around us. We upgrade our TV, mobile, AC, Car, refrigerator, laptop etc. But are we upgrading our mind and thought? Are we still old vine in old bottle? Is our mind and thinking centuries old? The more away you go from God and related blind faiths, the closer you will be to humans and humanity... and then you will realize that service to humanity is the greatest possible worship and devotion.

****

When surrounded by life's problems, people start running from pillar to post. from one temple to other and to Astrologers, mystics and liquor bars. But problems never vanish. They wait for them to come back to strike again. On their run people forget that they only must tackle their problems. If you have a strong and dedicated mindset, no problems can trouble you because you will always be ready to face and hit back. What we must develop is logical mind, not imaginative and sensitive mind.

Leucippus, a Greek philosopher said that everything is made of tiny particles called atoms in 5th century BC. But Sage Kanada said same thing in 2nd century BC. Aryabhata and Bhaskara propounded cosmic theories centuries before Bruno, Copernicus and Galileo. Bruno was burnt alive for telling that earth is round. Galileo was jailed for telling that earth is revolving around Sun. These were told centuries before by our rishis. Knowledge was advancing in ancient India when other parts of the world was in mental darkness.

****

Today's generation is living in Google Era. They are living with blank Minds. They are allergic to Books. No reading. It is unusual to find books in modern homes. Bookstalls are closing. A Google addicted generation is moving around with blank Minds. They will have no knowledge to pass on to their children. Children also will have to depend on Google. This will lead to communication gap between parents and children and they will fail to create emotional bond. Parents are primary role models in front of children. It's time everyone does introspection to see if they can be role models for next generation.

For deriving scientific proof, we must use scientific method of thinking and analyzing every event. The process of thinking must be critical/logical. We must analyze everything based on available knowledge. It is a critical process which involves careful analysis, evaluation and thinking and finally accepting or rejecting. To accept something blindly is the easiest activity. This is what most people do. World is full of mysteries. Science has unraveled most of the mysteries of yesterday. Today's mysteries may or may not be unraveled tomorrow. It is wiser to consider mysteries as mysteries instead of coloring or shadowing with some supernatural beliefs.

****

Religious faith has intoxication so it can continue to enslave humanity. But to be rational, one's thinking, and intellectual faculty must function. There is no intoxication here. Here it's intellect that motivates one to progress. Progress did not fall from sky. It's made by brainy humans

Corona virus is teaching us an unforgettable lession. That's of universal brotherhood. Virus did not see geographical boundaries, religions, races, color of skin. It has attacked the entire human race. None of the weapons man has in store is useful against this invisible enemy. The entire human community is now Jointly waging war against corona. It's time to give up all political and cultural differences join into a single global community to face all challenges of today and tomorrow. It's time to give up all fanaticism, terrorism and all rivalries. Or human race may be wiped out may be by another potent virus. Preservation of nature and thus retaining climatic conditions is necessary. Global warming, increasing pollution etc can encourage virus mutation. Retaining cleanliness and hygiene is another warning virus is giving us. We should treat every bit of surrounding as part of our home and do all that is possible to maintain cleanliness. Let us make ourselves proud that we are humans.

****

Are you about to buy some items? Planning to do interior designing on your house? Are you running pillar to post for opinions? Ten people will give ten different opinions? Confused? You failed to seek opinion of two important people. One you yourself and other one is expert in the field. Seeking your own opinion will be worthless if you don't have a knowledge base in your mind. In such cases go by expert opinion. Don't try to overrule expert's opinion with your immature views. Remember he has expertise in the field through his learning which you may not have.

SALUTE WOMEN on Women's Day – a poem

Bygone centuries saw the enslavement
she suffered at the hands of men.
In the name of religion, she was tortured,
enslaved and even burnt to death.
She is paraded naked and sold on the street,
to gratify the lust of men.
A few try to destroy her even in embryonic stage.
Day in and day out she is more harassed than loved,
by the men whom she gave birth.
But still she continues to serve him with love and care.
It is she who teaches him what loving, and caring is.
It is she who rare him and makes him great.
She is there behind each of his achievements.
We see her in Kiran Bedi * who is roaring against injustice.
We see her in Hellen Keller who defeated her blindness.
We see her in Florence Nightingale who nursed the humanity.
We also see her in Mother Teresa, the goddess of kindness.
If there is an adorable creature on earth,
It is only she, "the Woman"

[* Kiran Bedi is the first woman IPS officer of India.
She is the winner of Magsaysay Award.]

"LIFELESS EARTH -- a poem

Man continue to be selfish,
Aggressive, intolerant and corrupt,
Peace and harmony are lost from world,
Man try to eliminate his own race,
An act animal is ashamed to do!
Money which could wipe out poverty,
Is spent to mound atomic weapons,
Not to protect us from aliens,
But to eliminate our own species.
Love is lost, hatred is on forefront,
Peace is nowhere, war cries all over,
Life is in peril, explosions continue to rock,
When faith and religion flourish,
Humans become endangered species.
Faith and devotion to God,
which existed since time immemorial,
Could not turn man into humane.
And beautiful earth is slowly turning,
To a museum of the dead.
The sun will soon be very sad,
To have a lifeless earth
Revolving round it."

LIFE- A MIRACLE OF NATURE—a poem

"Life, a miracle of nature,
an evolved molecule of matter,
blossomed in the vast expanse of oceans.
Methane, ammonia, hydrogen and water vapor
When joined under the radio-active sun,
The molecules of nonliving matter underwent
massive changes and became live.
It's this accident that made the molecule of protein,
Which even Stanley Miller reproduced in lab.
Evolution went on, and on and changed,
from amoeba to dinosaurs, from ape to man,
It was an amazing architecture of nature,
Which continue improving human brain.
The amazing creation of nature, the man,
kept on exploring the mysteries of nature,
and succeeded in duplicating nature's marvel
through his latest invention - the cloning,
and succeeded in decoding even the genetic code.
Still we must salute the mother nature,
which has many more mysteries in store!"

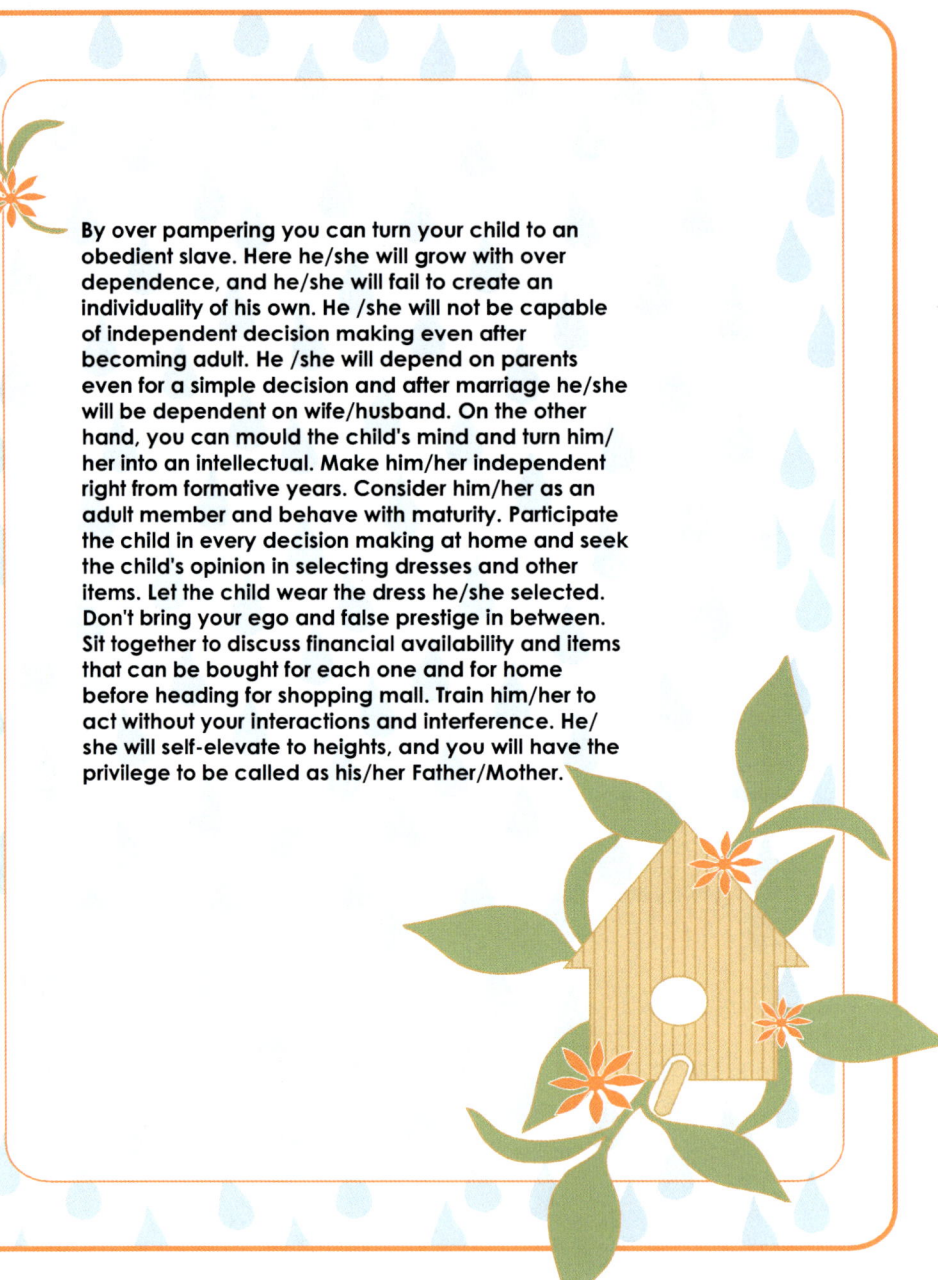

By over pampering you can turn your child to an obedient slave. Here he/she will grow with over dependence, and he/she will fail to create an individuality of his own. He /she will not be capable of independent decision making even after becoming adult. He /she will depend on parents even for a simple decision and after marriage he/she will be dependent on wife/husband. On the other hand, you can mould the child's mind and turn him/her into an intellectual. Make him/her independent right from formative years. Consider him/her as an adult member and behave with maturity. Participate the child in every decision making at home and seek the child's opinion in selecting dresses and other items. Let the child wear the dress he/she selected. Don't bring your ego and false prestige in between. Sit together to discuss financial availability and items that can be bought for each one and for home before heading for shopping mall. Train him/her to act without your interactions and interference. He/she will self-elevate to heights, and you will have the privilege to be called as his/her Father/Mother.

Once I was walking towards my flat after going for shopping. I saw my friend coming from opposite direction. He was walking at moderate speed. As he approached near me, he was looking at me. I said good morning. He did not reciprocate and walked ahead. If such an incident happens, what do you feel? He never bothered not only to speak, by he ignored. In the evening I phoned him and asked, "How are you? Where were you going in the morning?"

"I was going to the hospital. One of my colleagues is sick", he replied. "But how did you know that?", he asked me. I did not tell that I saw him.
Though his eyes were seeing me, his mind was not. Many such small incidents lead to misunderstanding. Keep your mind always awake so that your five senses bring you correct information. Your senses can perceive without your conscious knowledge. Such perceptions need not be correct. These are called deceptive perceptions. Whatever you see in a magic show are not real. But you feel they are real. You can have deceptive perception due to blind beliefs. If oxygen supply to brain reduces, then too one may experience such things. Many agencies and individuals can take advantage of this to make money.

Once I was walking towards my flat after going for shopping. I saw my friend coming from opposite direction. He was walking at moderate speed. As he approached near me, he was looking at me. I said good morning. He did not reciprocate and walked ahead. If such an incident happens, what do you feel? He never bothered not only to speak, by he ignored. In the evening I phoned him and asked, "How are you? Where were you going in the morning?"

"I was going to the hospital. One of my colleagues is sick", he replied. "But how did you know that?", he asked me. I did not tell that I saw him.

Though his eyes were seeing me, his mind was not. Many such small incidents lead to misunderstanding. Keep your mind always awake so that your five senses bring you correct information. Your senses can perceive without your conscious knowledge. Such perceptions need not be correct. These are called deceptive perceptions. Whatever you see in a magic show are not real. But you feel they are real. You can have deceptive perception due to blind beliefs. If oxygen supply to brain reduces, then too one may experience such things. Many agencies and individuals can take advantage of this to make money.

When dog see food, it starts salivating. Nobel prize winning physiologist Ivan Pavlov rang a bell every time he gave food to his dog. After repeating for many days, once he only rang the bell but didn't bring food. On hearing the bell, the dog started salivating. Here an association between food and bell sound was formed in the dog's brain. Pavlov called this Conditioned Reflex. Since childhood many such conditioned reflexes are formed in our mind. This influences our habit and behaviour.

Looking auspicious time, direction we keep our head while sleeping, direction of kitchen platform, using right hand while giving something to someone, looking for vastu, directions etc while buying flats. People blindly adhere to all though there is no scientific basis. They are not able to break the conditioned reflex formed in their mind which require conscious effort. They continue with these throughout their life. They create many such conditioned reflexes in their children's mind too.

Are you a sleeping doll, sleeping on and off? Sleep is lingering in you even when you are awake. Look in the mirror. Your face shows you are lethargic and tired! Extra dose of sleep turns you lethargic, dormant and kills your self-confidence. It turns you into a doll who always need other's help to turn alive. You literally become a puppet who can never do or decide anything own your own. Sleep is a form of rest which automatically takes over you when your body and brain cells are tired. It comes to you automatically. You need not invite or forcibly Bring. It does not need darkness or sound proofing. Sleep is complete if you feel fresh and vibrant at wakeup. For this you should schedule your sleep time and pattern as per your work schedule. While sleep requirements vary slightly from person to person, healthy adults need between 7 to 8 hours of sleep per night to function at their best. Children and teens need even more. And despite the notion that our sleep needs decrease with age, most older people still need at least 7 hours of sleep. If you have symptoms of anxiety or psychosis, you can have sleep disturbance for which you should take psychiatric help. Ensure that sleep makes you wake up energetic, vibrant and joyful.

Made in the USA
Columbia, SC
29 November 2022

46e56e17-0ec9-4c5f-932f-9cf0703c9257R17